# How to Make Things Grow

by DAVID WICKERS and JOHN TUEY

illustrated with
photographs and drawings

SCHOLASTIC BOOK SERVICES
NEW YORK • TORONTO • LONDON • AUCKLAND • SYDNEY • TOKYO

Acknowledgements

Drawings and diagrams by Sharon Finmark.
Photos: pages 8 and 20, Sutton and Sons Ltd;
page 29, Fisons Ltd, Garden Products.

This book is sold subject to the condition that it shall not be resold, lent, or otherwise circulated in any binding or cover other than that in which it is published — unless prior written permission has been obtained from the publisher — and without a similar condition, including this condition, being imposed on the subsequent purchaser.

Copyright© 1972 by David Wickers and John Tuey. This edition is published by Scholastic Book Services, a division of Scholastic Magazines, Inc., by arrangement with Van Nostrand Reinhold Company.

1st printing . . . . . . . . . . . . . . . . . . . . . . . . . . . . . . . . . . . . . . . . . . . . . . . . . . . . . . . . . . . . . March 1975

Printed in the U.S.A.

# Contents

Introduction    4

Find out about plants
    Plants and water    5
    Plants and sunlight    8
    Plants and air    10
    Plants and movement    12
    Plants and soil    16
    Plants and reproduction    18

How to start planting and sowing
    Indoor bulbs    21
    Sowing seeds from packets    24
    Mustard farm    26
    Planting fruit pits    27
    Transplanting    28
    Cuttings    28

Making things grow indoors
    "Green hair"    30
    Potato plants    31
    Looking after house plants    32
    Miniature garden    34
    Miniature desert    38
    Underwater garden    40
    Bottle garden    42

Making things grow out of doors
    Window boxes    44
    Preparing the ground    46
    Weed garden    48
    Flower Garden    48
    Vegetable Garden    52
    Hanging Garden    54

Hints for outdoor gardens    56

Flowers to grow from seeds    60

Index    62

# Introduction

In order to make things grow successfully, you should first know a few basic facts about plants. This book starts with six experiments for you to try for yourself, each of which will tell you a little more about how plants behave.

This is a book for everyone. If you live in a tall apartment house in the city, you can still have gardens inside your home and display them in all manner of settings. And if you make a garden of your own, you will soon learn to apply the simple gardening techniques in this book that will help you grow things successfully.

Everyone can have those magical green fingers. You can bring color to the dullest patch of ground, or the greenery of the countryside to your city windowsills.

# Find out about plants

**Plants and water**

You need:
potato, knife, bowl, white carnation, red and blue ink, 2 glasses, potted geranium, clear plastic bag, string

1. Scrape the peel from one half of the potato and cut a slice off that end to give it a flat base.

2. Cut a hollow down into the center of the potato at the opposite end.

3. Stand the potato in the bowl on its flat end and fill the bowl with enough water to cover the peeled area. Then watch what happens.

The water will begin to rise through tiny membranes in the potato and slowly fill the hollow in the top. This is very similar to the way in which water and minerals from the soil travel up the roots of a plant. Scientists call this process "osmosis."

1. Carefully cut along the lower half of the stem of the white carnation so that it divides in two.

2. Pour some red ink in one glass and blue ink in the other. Add some water to dilute the inks.

3. Stand the flower in the two glasses, with one half of the stem in the red ink and the other in the blue.

After a while, the carnation will become half red and half blue! Water is drawn up from both glasses through tiny tube-like cells in the stem to the flower itself. Even giant trees draw water from the ground up to their leaves in the same way.

The water that is drawn up from the roots and through the stem of a plant passes out into the atmosphere through minute holes in the leaves. This is called "transpiration."

1. Place a clear plastic bag over the potted geranium and tie it around the stem with string so that air cannot enter.

2. Water the plant and place it in the sun.

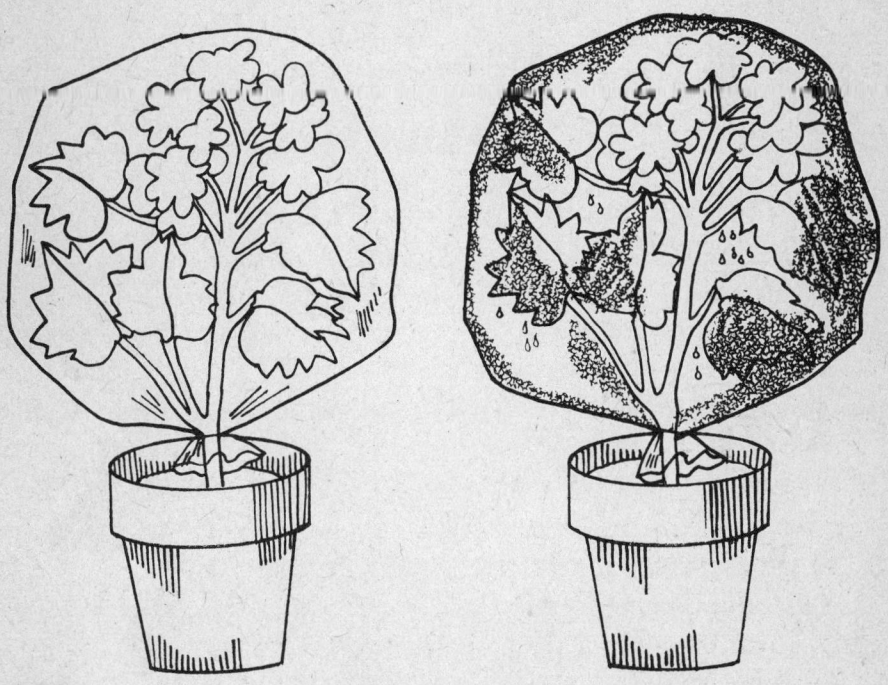

After a few hours remove the bag. The inside will be coated with water. This is moisture that has been drawn up from the soil and *transpired* by the leaves into the air.

**Plants and sunlight**

You need:
a geranium (or other green plant), aluminum foil, saucer, teaspoon, ethyl alcohol, paper clips, diluted iodine

1. Attach a strip of aluminum foil to the upper surface of one of the geranium leaves with some paper clips.

2. Keep the plant in a sunny place for two to three days.

3. Remove the partly covered leaf and take off the foil. Soak the leaf in alcohol for a few hours to take away some of the green coloring (the chlorophyll).

4. Put a few drops of iodine on the leaf with the teaspoon, and watch what happens. (Iodine is one of a number of liquids that react in one way to a substance that contains starch and in a different way to any substance that does not. Chemists can use it to find out whether or not starch is present.)

The parts of the leaf that were not covered by the foil will turn dark blue and show that starch is present. The covered part that did not get any sunlight will turn brown and show that this area lacks starch.

All green plants need sunlight in order to live. The sun supplies energy with which they make their own food or "starch" from the carbon dioxide in air and in water. This process is called "photosynthesis," meaning "light to build with," and occurs because of the green "chlorophyll" substance in the leaves.

Starch is present in many of the foods we eat. If you peel and grate some potatoes, wrap the peel in a handkerchief, and then squeeze it underwater, a powder will appear. Leave it to settle and pour away the water. When you test the powder with iodine you can prove that it is starch.

## Plants and air

You need:
a green water weed
large glass jar
plastic funnel
test tube
taper or long thin,
   dry stick
matches

1. Fill the jar with water. Place the water plant on the bottom and cover it with the funnel.

2. Fill the test tube with water. Put your thumb over the open end to avoid spilling the water and turn it upside down. Lower the end of the tube into the jar and fit it over the spout of the funnel.

3. Place the jar in the sunlight. Tiny bubbles of gas from the weed will gather at the top of the test tube and begin to push the water out.

4. When all the water has left the test tube, take it off the funnel, keeping your thumb over the end to prevent any gas escaping. Ask an adult to light the stick or taper. Hold it and let it burn for a few seconds, and then blow out the flame. Quickly remove your thumb from the test tube and put the end of the stick into the tube. Then watch what happens.

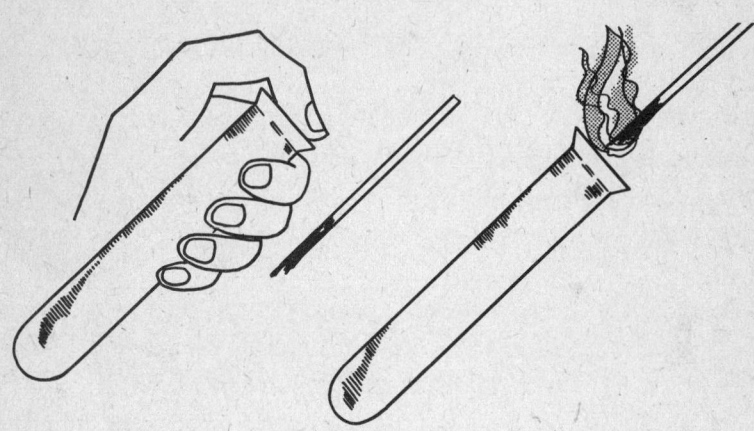

The stick or taper will relight when it enters the test tube. This shows that the gas in the test tube was pure oxygen ("ordinary" air contains only about one-fifth oxygen). During photosynthesis plants produce oxygen and help to keep the balance of oxygen and carbon dioxide in the air. And so plants not only provide food for animals and humans but also oxygen for them to breathe.

## Plants and movement

You need:
cotton
glass coffee jar
bean seeds
clay pot
2 large cardboard boxes
potting soil
drinking straw
2 thick books
potted geranium
sand
scissors
flower pot
thread
pin
piece of cardboard 8½" x 11"

1. Fill the coffee jar with wet cotton and slip the bean seeds between the cotton and the sides of the jar.

2. After a few days roots will begin to grow downward from the beans. If you turn the jar upside down and leave it for another few days, the roots will change direction and begin to grow downward again.

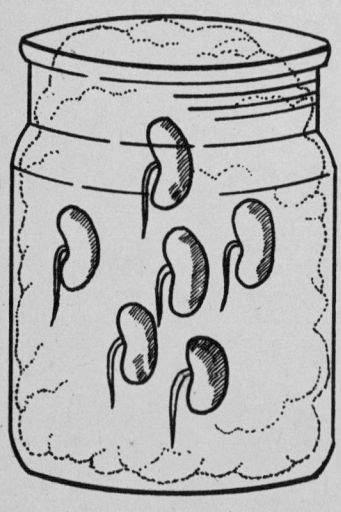 

Roots are attracted down toward the earth because of the force of gravity. This is known as "geotropism." In their search for water, however, roots do not always grow downward.

1. Fill one large cardboard box with sand or potting soil and push the clay pot down into the center. Fill the pot with water.

2. Use the bean seeds from the last experiment and plant the *roots* in the sand or potting soil around the pot, leaving the *beans* on the surface.

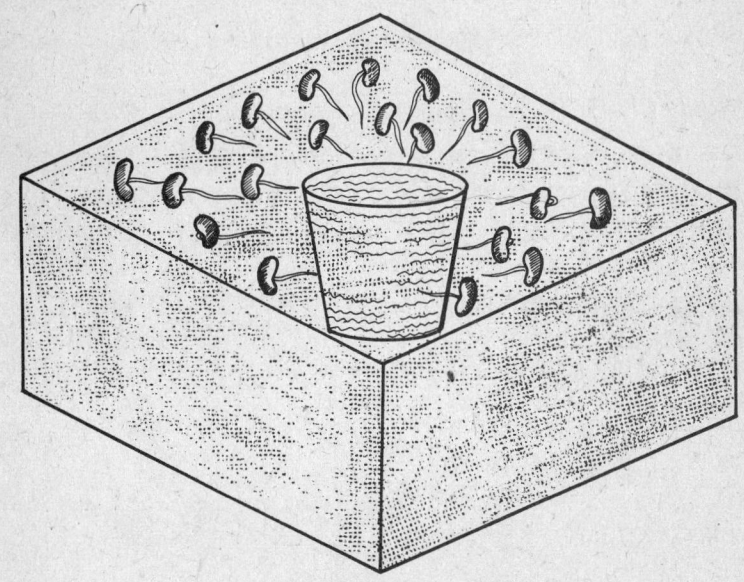

After a few days, carefully brush away the sand or potting soil around the beans and you will see that the roots have begun to grow sideways toward the water. This movement is called "hydrotropism."

Unlike the roots, the shoots themselves will grow toward the light they require for photosynthesis.

1. Stand the other cardboard box upright and cut a hole in one side almost at the top. Put the potted geranium inside and then close the box.

2. Stand the box in a sunny place with the hole pointing toward the sun. In a short while the geranium will begin to lean toward the hole in order to get sunlight.

3. Turn the geranium around in the box. The same thing will happen — the geranium will change position and lean toward the sunlight once more.

You have seen geotropism and hydrotropism in action — the movement of plants toward the light is called "phototropism."

You can also watch the rate at which plants grow, as well as the direction.

1. Soak a bean seed in water for a few hours and then plant it in a flowerpot filled with potting soil.

2. When the shoot first appears, tie one end of a short length of thread around it. Tie the other end of the thread around the tip of a drinking straw.

3. Stand the cardboard upright between two thick books and place the pot alongside. Pull the thread taut and pin the straw to the cardboard as shown, fairly near the knot, so that it points upward.

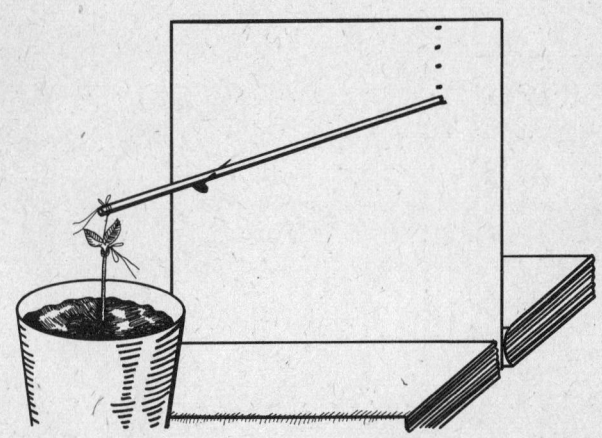

As the shoot grows, it will lift one end of the straw. The free end of the straw will move down the card. Make a mark against it at the same time each day so you can see how fast the plant is growing.

## Plants and soil

You need:
screw-topped jar
soil from the garden
spade
2 tin cans
2 beans

1. Half fill the jar with garden soil.

2. Fill it to the top with water, replace the cap, and shake it around.

Let the jar stand. You will see that the soil separates into different layers. The heavy particles, such as gravel and sand, will sink to the bottom. Next will come a layer of clay. The water itself will remain cloudy because very fine particles of clay are floating in it. On the surface you will see small, floating particles called "humus." This is made up of plant and animal matter which has been decayed by bacteria in the soil to make room for new plants, and provide valuable minerals on which the growing plants feed.

The soil you used is called "topsoil" because it is found near the surface. Put some in one of the cans. Dig about 1½ feet beneath the earth's surface and put some of this "subsoil" in the other can. Soak two bean seeds overnight in water and plant one in each can. Keep both of them moist.

When the seedlings begin to grow, the bean planted in the topsoil will look much healthier than the one growing in the subsoil. The subsoil is less "fertile" because it contains less humus than the topsoil.

As well as providing minerals for plants, the soil also acts as a reservoir of water for the roots, holds them in place, and allows air to reach them.

**Plants and reproduction**

You need:
a knife and a magnifying glass

Most plants produce seeds from which new plants can grow after their "parent" plant has withered and died.

To produce fertile seeds, pollen from the stamen (the male part of the plant) has to be transferred to the pistil (the female part of the plant which contains the seeds). Soon after they have been fertilized in this way, the seeds are ready to leave the parent plant so that a few, in turn, will germinate, grow into plants, and then produce their own seeds.

Look closely at a flower and try to pick out all the different parts that perform the work of pollination. The brightly colored petals (**a**) attract insects, such as wasps and bees, that look for nectar. These help to transfer the pollen, sometimes from the stamen (**b**) to the pistil (**c**) of the same plant, but usually they carry the pollen on their bodies from one plant to another. At the bottom of the pistil is the ovary (**d**). Carefully cut this in half and you will see all the seeds inside.

Seeds may be scattered in various ways. They may be carried by the wind, like the dandelion (**e**), or the sycamore (**f**) whose seeds have wings; they may hook onto the fur of animals, like the burdock (**g**); they may float away on the surface of the water, like the water lily; they may shoot out from a pod (**h**) when it dries and splits open; and so on.

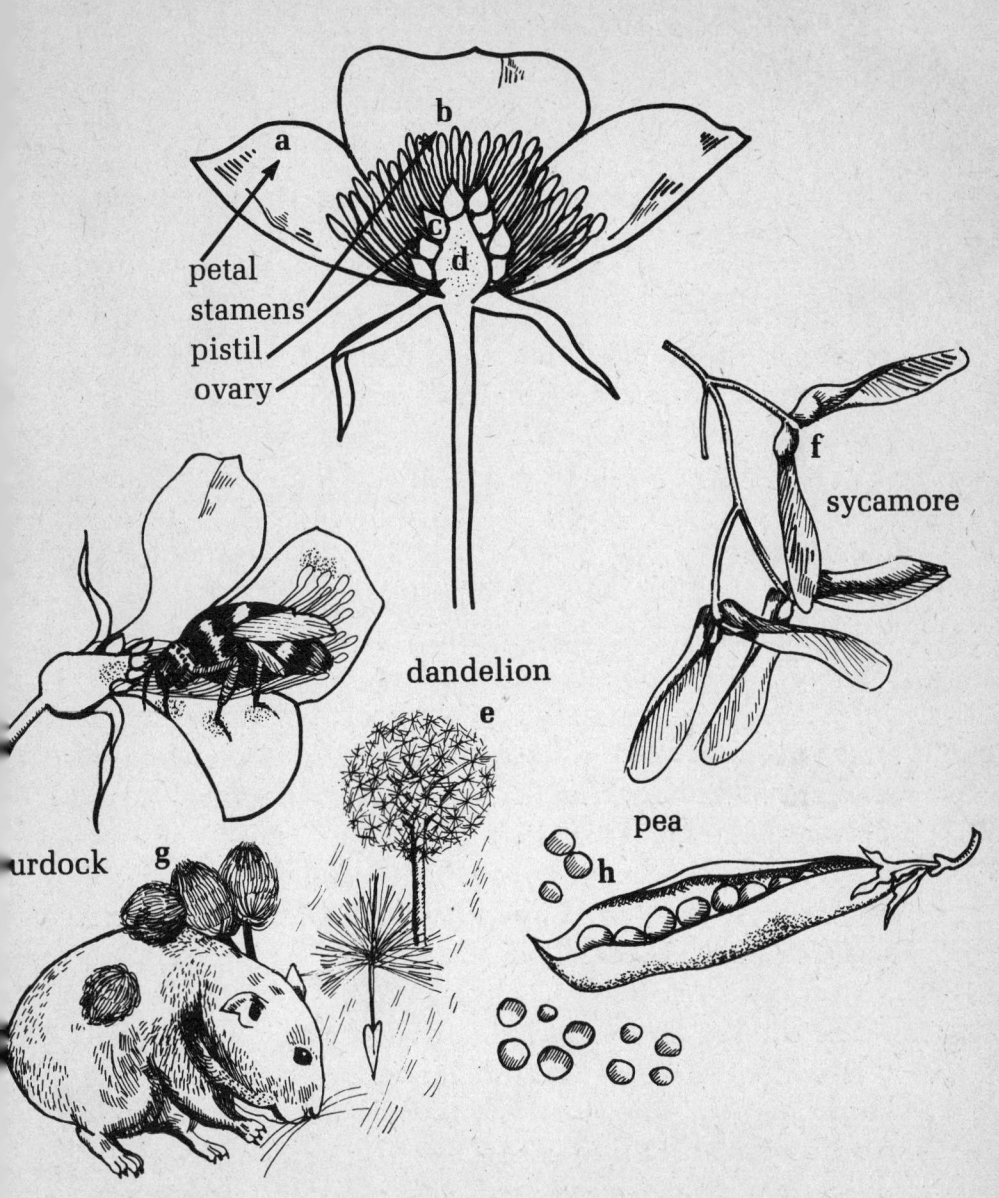

# How to start planting and sowing

Not all plants start as seeds from flowers. Some grow from another kind of seed — the pits we find inside fruit. Yet others start as bulbs or corms that look rather like onions and grow near the roots of the parent plant.

The best time to plant bulbs is in the autumn. They will grow throughout the winter and flower in the spring. You can plant them in the garden or in a bowl indoors.

**Indoor bulbs**

You need:
a large bowl, peat moss and bulbs (from garden shops or chain stores), bucket

1. Put the peat moss into the bucket and fill it up with water. Leave it to soak overnight.

2. Squeeze out as much water from the moss as you can with your fingers and half fill the bowl. Do this over some old newspaper in case you make a mess.

3. Set the bulbs upright on the peat moss. (The top is usually slightly pointed and the bottom is flatter, with traces of roots on it.) Arrange the bulbs in groups but not too close together or their roots will tangle.

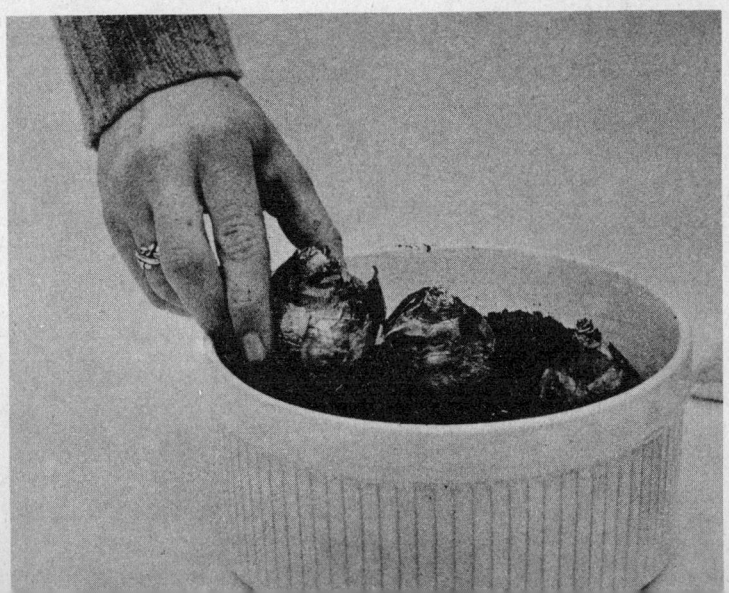

4. Fill up the space in between the bulbs with peat moss and press it down with your fingers. Leave the tops of the bulbs sticking out above the surface.

5. Place the bowl in a dark cellar or cupboard for two months. Keep the peat moss moist (but do not over water) and make sure the plants have plenty of air.

6. After two months, by which time the roots will have grown, bring the bulbs out into the light. Place them on a windowsill so that they get plenty of sun, and keep the peat moss moist.

You can also grow bulbs with just pebbles, charcoal and water—or even just water—in the bowl.

Bulbs and corms are really stores of food (sugar and starch) which enable the plant to grow. An onion is a bulb. If you cut one in half (**a**) you will see the new flower bud surrounded by the scale leaves. When they have fed the plant they wither and turn into the brown, thin covering that surrounds the onion. A parent plant forms bulbs underground at the base of its stem.

Corms are similar to bulbs. They are a store of food for the growing plant, but when you cut one in half (**b**) you will see that it does not have scale leaves like a bulb. It is really part of the stem that grows fat with its reserves of food. A crocus is a corm (**c**).

*Types of bulbs to grow:* Narcissus (the daffodil is a narcissus), snowdrops, tulips, hyacinth.
*Types of corms to grow:* Crocus, gladioli, freesia.

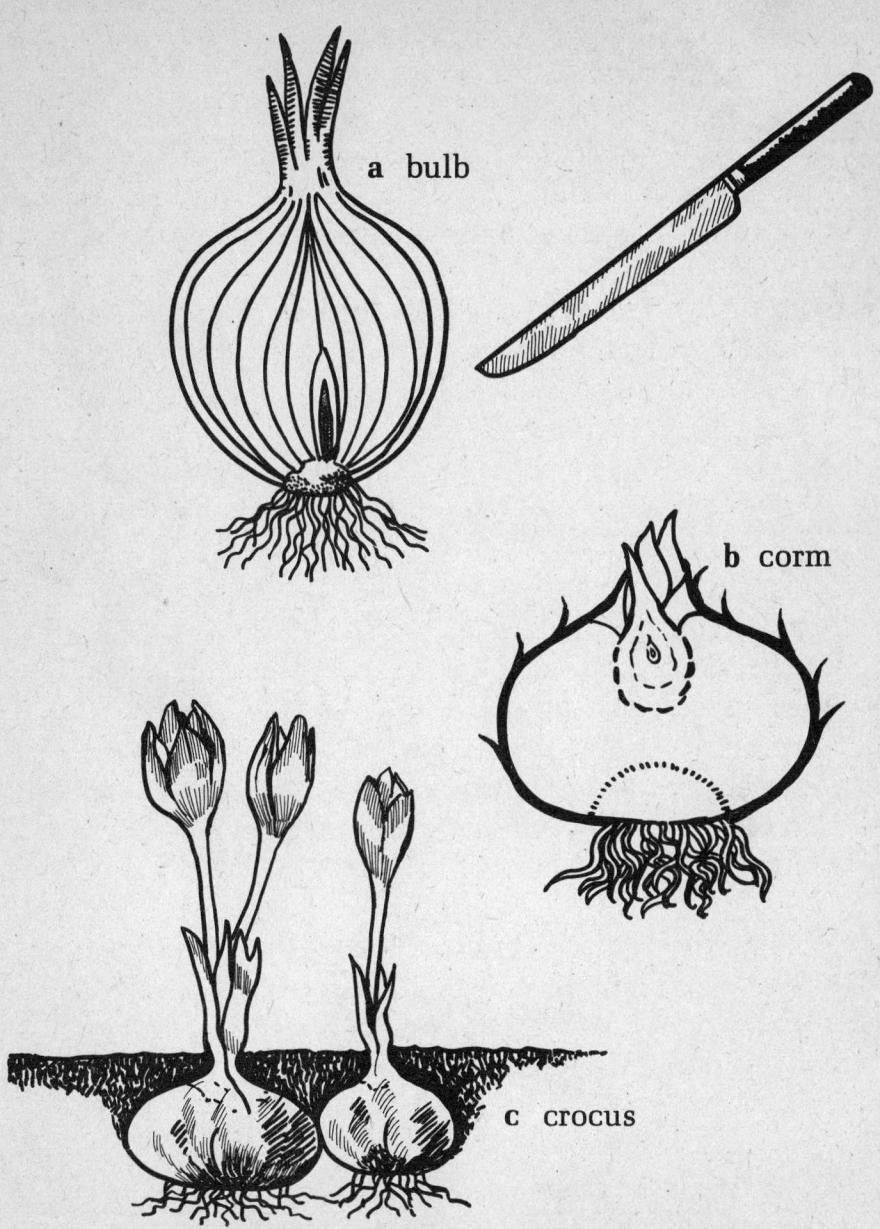

## Sowing seeds from packets

You need:
aluminum-foil pans, from
   pies or frozen foods
potting soil, from a
   garden shop
large dishes

large plastic bags
small watering can
knitting needle
variety of seeds
small corks

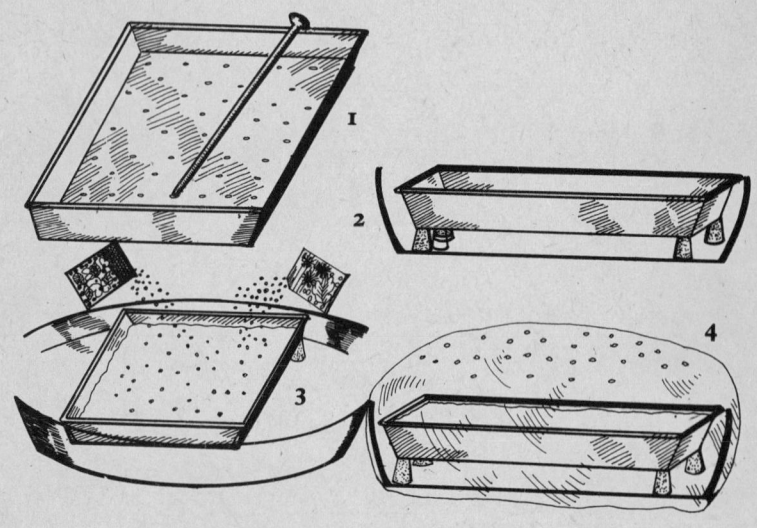

1. Punch some holes in the bottom of each pan with the knitting needle.

2. Fill each pan nearly to the top with potting soil and press down lightly. Place each pan in a dish with a cork under each corner of the pan.

3. Sprinkle a few seeds on the surface and cover them with a very thin layer of soil. Press down lightly.

4. Soak the soil with water. Punch some holes in the plastic bags with the knitting needle. Place them over the seed trays and tuck them around the dishes.

5. Keep the soil moist while the seeds are growing, but take care not to let the water that comes out through the drainage holes and into the dish rise to the bottom of the pans. The pans must not sit in water.

When the seeds begin to sprout, place the dishes close to a window so that they get plenty of sun.

Each seed contains a tiny store of food which nourishes the plant until the roots and leaves have grown big enough to support it.

You might also like to try growing seeds in eggshells filled with potting soil and placed in the egg box.

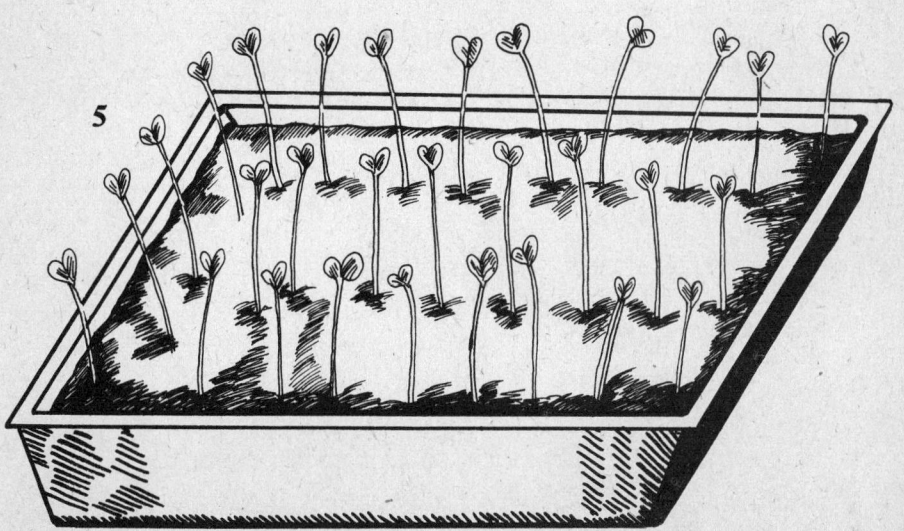

## Mustard farm

You need:
paper towels, a saucer, mustard seeds

1. Place a few paper towels in the saucer and soak them with water. Sprinkle the mustard seeds on the towels, and keep moist.

2. Keep the saucer in front of a window.

In about two weeks you will have fresh mustard to put in your sandwiches or salad.

Using the same method you can also grow the bean sprouts that you eat at Chinese restaurants. They are called "Mung beans" and you can buy the seeds in packets.

## Planting fruit pits

Fruit pits are also seeds but because of their size it is better to grow them in small pots.

1. Soak a few pits in water overnight. (You could use orange, lemon, grapefruit, melon, cherry, grape or apple pits.)

2. Place a few stones or pieces of broken clay pot in the bottom of some flowerpots. (You could use yoghurt containers instead, with a hole punched in the bottom.) Fill them almost to the top with potting soil.

3. Press one or two pits into each pot. Stand the pots in a saucer and keep the soil moist. Keep them away from direct sunlight until they begin to sprout.

## Transplanting

When the seeds have grown into seedlings, they should be replanted—either in the garden or in larger pots—to give them more room to grow.

Carefully turn one of the small pots upside down, holding the stem of the seedling lightly between the fingers of one hand. Tap the rim of the pot on the edge of a table. The plant will slide out, still firmly rooted in a ball of soil like the pot plant in the photograph. (If you transplant from the seed trays, carefully lift the seedlings out with the soil still around their roots using an old spoon.) Put some soil in the bottom of a larger pot, place the seedling in the middle, and fill up the rest of the space with soil (a). Press the surface down firmly with your fingers.

If you replant the seedlings in the garden, dig a small hole with a trowel or old spoon, pour in some water, place the ball of soil in the hole, and press the ground firmly around it (b). Give the seedlings plenty of water at first and then keep the soil moist.

## Cuttings

You can also grow some plants—roses, geraniums, chrysanthemums, and apple, for example—by taking "cuttings" from older, fully grown plants.

Geraniums are the easiest to grow in this way. Being very careful, cut a newly grown side shoot from the main stem of the plant at the place where they join (c). Remove the leaves from the lower half (d) and push the shoot deeply into some potting soil (e). Keep the soil moist but not wet.

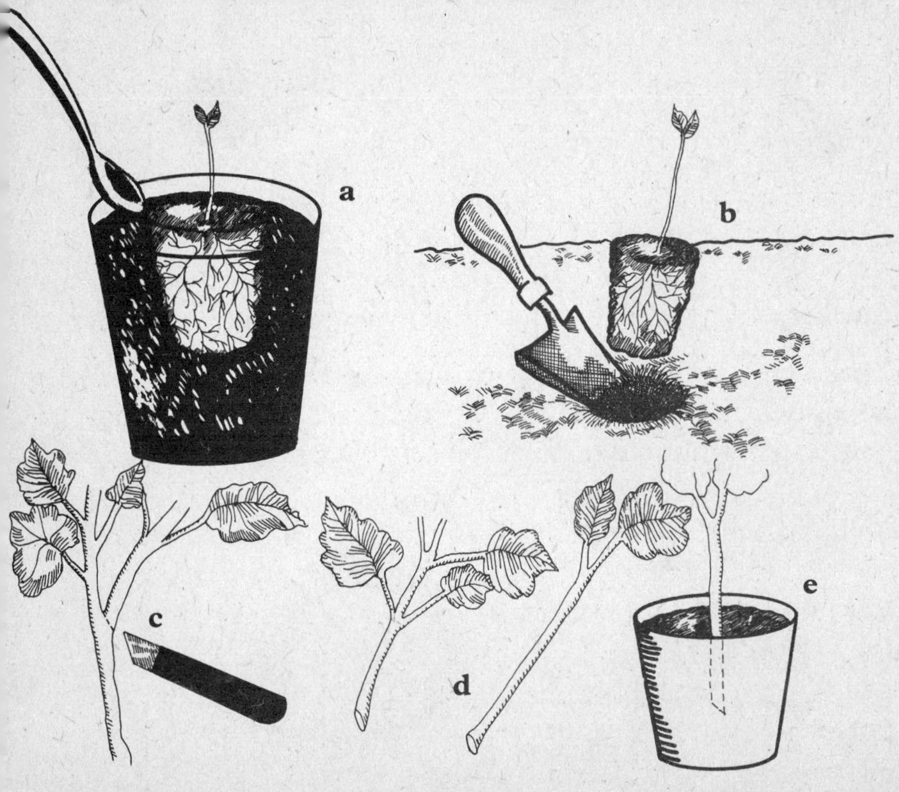

# Making things grow indoors

**"Green hair"**

You need:
clay flowerpot, dish, colored crayons, grass seed, soil

1. Turn the flowerpot upside down and draw a face on one side with the crayons.

2. Place the flowerpot in the dish. Put a thin layer of soil on the top of the pot and cover it with grass seeds, pressing them gently in place. Keep the dish filled with water.

   The water will soak up through the porous pot, and the grass will grow longer and longer on top of the "head." Don't forget to give it a haircut sometimes!

## Potato plants

You need:
potato, 4 toothpicks, jar, flowerpots, potting soil, knife

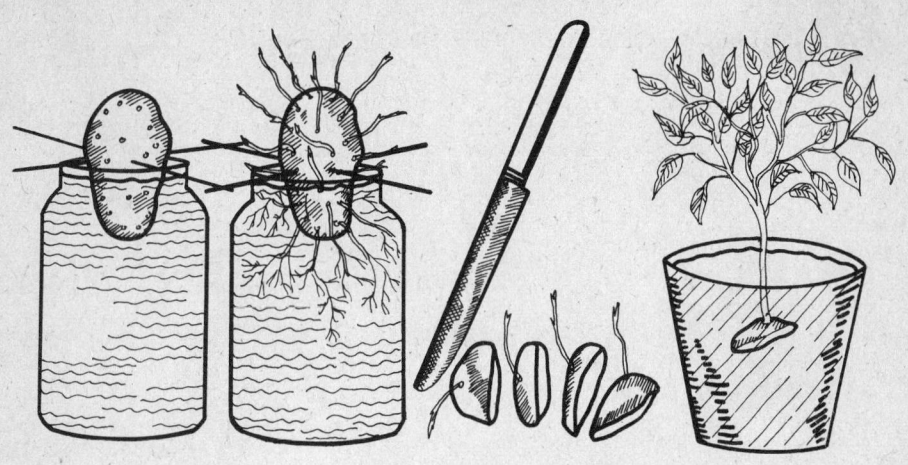

1. Push four toothpicks into a potato so that they form a cross. Fill a jar with water and place half of the potato, supported on the jar by the sticks, in the water.

2. Keep the jar filled with water and after a week or so roots and shoots will grow from the "eyes."

3. When the shoots have grown a little, remove the potato from the jar and cut it into pieces, each with its own shoot. Plant each piece in a pot, well covered with soil. Keep the soil moist and soon you will have a full-fledged potato plant.

## Looking after house plants

Individually potted house plants are the most common form of indoor plants. Some can be grown from seeds or cuttings, but it is better to buy the young plants, already potted, from garden or chain stores.

Among the easiest to keep are: ivy, rubber plant (**a**), snake plant (**e**), spider plant, wandering Jew (**b**), philodendron (**c**), geranium, impatiens (**d**), and coleus.

Most of these come from the tropics, so it is important that you keep them in a room where the temperature remains warm and even. (The kitchen, for example, is a bad place to keep plants because of temperature variations and the cooking fumes.)

Keep the plants on the windowsill, but do not place them in direct sunlight. Water them about twice a week in spring and summer when they are growing vigorously, but only occasionally in the winter months when they are almost dormant.

a  b  c  d  e

House plants do not get washed by the rain, which keeps the leaf pores of outdoor plants clear so that they can "breathe." It is important, therefore, to dust and sponge the leaves of house plants from time to time.

When the plants have grown too large for their pots, you should transplant them to larger pots, as described on page 28.

Many of the plants in the list on the opposite page are climbers. In their natural state they grow toward the sun by attaching themselves around other plants and using them as ladders. You can build a lattice framework for your climbers to grow on, using split canes or sticks, tied together with string or wire.

## Minature garden

You need:
aluminum-foil baking pan, potting soil, seedlings, pebbles, charcoal

1. When the spring comes, start some seedlings from cherry pits, acorns, orange, lemon, and grapefruit pits, or any other seeds you can find. Instructions are on pages 24–25 and 27.

2. When the seedlings have grown, place a layer of pebbles and some pieces of charcoal in the bottom of the baking pan. This will act as a water reservoir to keep the soil from becoming too soggy. Fill the rest of the pan almost to the top with potting soil.

3. You can now begin to plant your miniature garden. Transplant the largest seedlings from the pots to the pan (described on page 28) so that they form a row along one side.

4. The smaller seedlings can be planted in the rest of the pan, but allow room in between each plant for the roots to grow.

5. You can even plant small twigs of ash, box, apple, and so on, which will grow to look like miniature trees. If you want to grow flowers, buy the seeds of small Alpine plants or miniature roses.

6. Sow grass seed in the spaces between the plants.

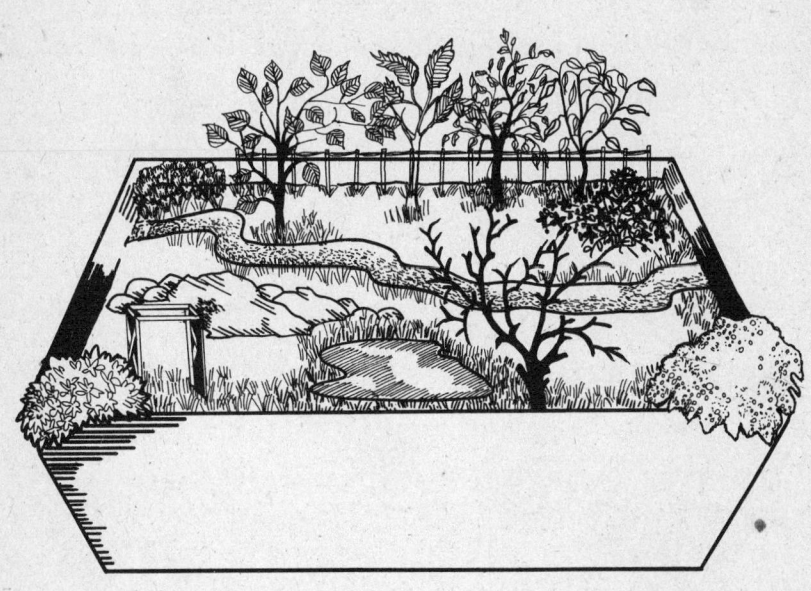

To make your miniature garden look realistic you could easily make some of the following "extras."

**a** *Paths:* These can be made from gravel or sand laid neatly on the grass (when it has begun to grow) in narrow lines.

**b** *Ponds:* Use small mirrors with a border of gravel, or even dishes pushed into the soil and filled with water.

**c** *Arches:* You can make an arch from narrow strips of balsa wood. Draw a full-size plan of the arch on a piece of paper. Cut the balsa wood into the same lengths as on the plan. Glue the pieces together.

**d** *Fences:* Just push a row of used matchsticks into the soil, head-first, and join them all together with a length of thread.

Place the pan on a table near the window, with the larger plants at the back. Water the miniature garden just enough to keep the surface always moist.

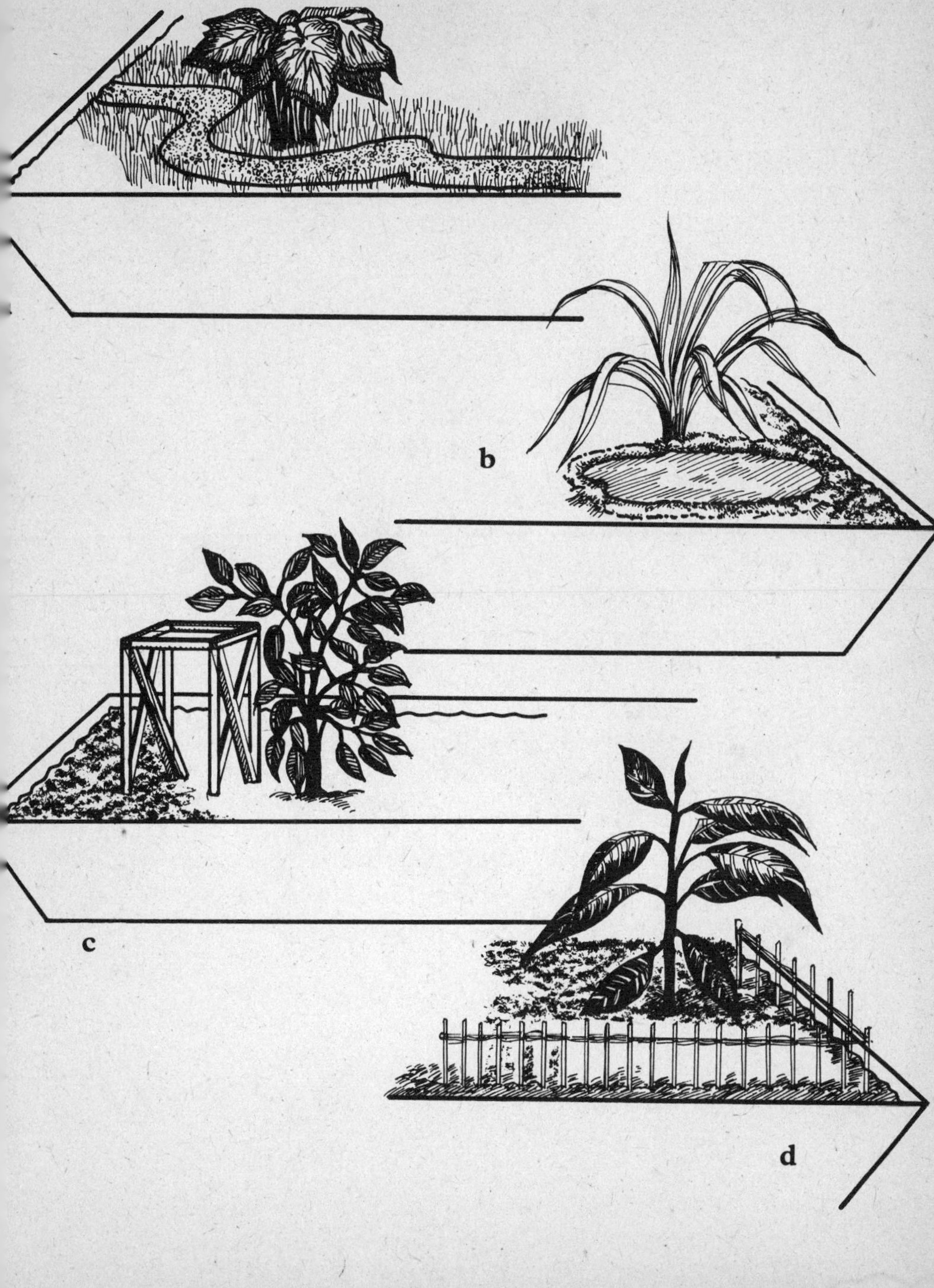
b
c
d

**Miniature desert**

You need:
aluminum-foil baking pan, potting soil, thin cardboard, cactus plants, sand, paints, scissors

1. Mix together equal quantities of potting soil and sand until you have almost enough to fill the pan.

2. Buy a selection of small, inexpensive cacti from a garden supplier. Transplant them from their pots into the mixture of soil and sand. Read page 28 to find out how to do this.

3. Cover the surface completely with a thin layer of sand.

4. Cut a piece of cardboard about 6 inches wide, and long enough to wrap around three sides of the pan. Paint a desert landscape right across it, with mountains, the sun, and other cacti in the distance.

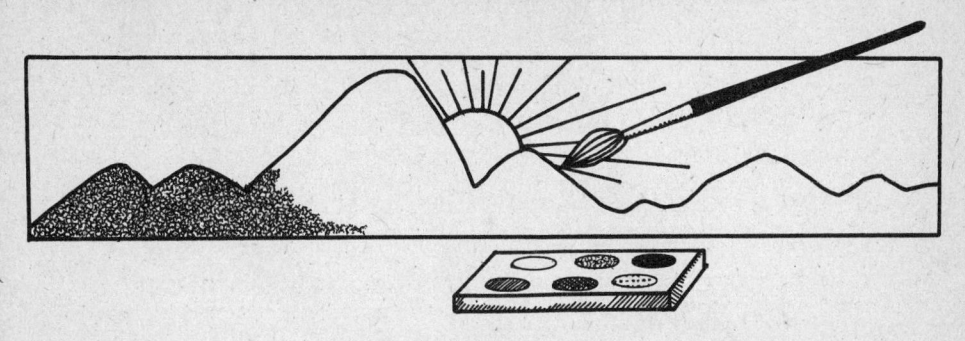

5. Push the lower edge of the card into the soil along the sides of the pan. You could also add a few small rocks, or a cabin made from matches or drinking straws, to the desert scene.

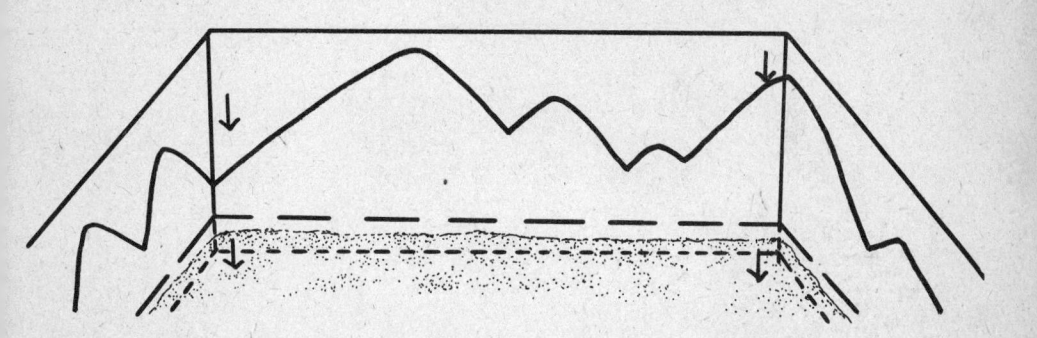

Keep the minature desert in the warmest room of the house, and in a place where it will get plenty of sun. You only need to water the cacti occasionally because they come from dry, hot desert regions and are able to store water for a long time in their fat stems.

Not all plants grow on dry land. The sea, ponds, rivers, and lakes all contain many types of plants especially adapted for life in the water. Some float freely on the surface, drawing food from the water and drifting with the current. Others are rooted in sand and mud beds and grow toward the surface to get light for "photosynthesis." With these plants you can grow an underwater garden, using an aquarium or even a large glass dish or jar.

**Underwater garden**

You need:
glass aquarium or large jar, potting soil, sand, pencil, water plants from a pet shop

1. Cover the bottom of the aquarium with a layer of sand about 1 inch deep. Cover the sand with a layer of potting soil about the same thickness, and then, on top of this, add another thin layer of sand.

2. Fill the aquarium with water from a jug. Take special care not to disturb the sand when you pour water onto it. Allow the sand plenty of time to settle.

3. Use a pencil to make small holes down into the sand at the bottom of the aquarium. Push the roots of the plants into the holes and carefully press the soil and sand back around the base of the plants.

You can buy water plants in any pet shop that stocks aquariums or you can collect your own plants from ponds and streams. Water hyacinth, floating moss, arrowhead, pondweed, water lilies, and duckweed are all suitable for an underwater garden.

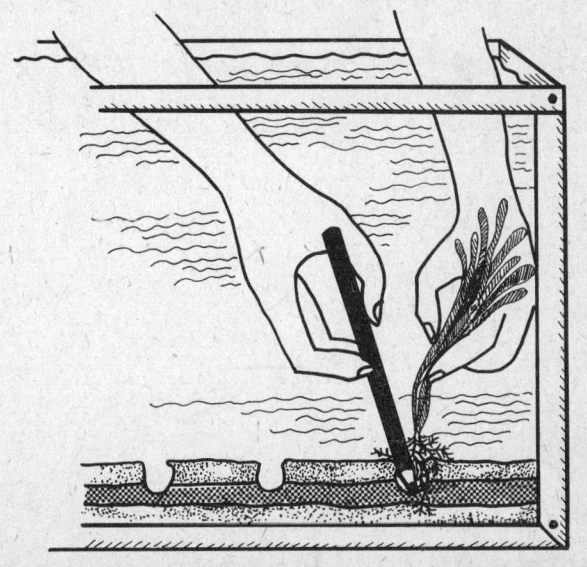

## Bottle garden

You need:
a large glass jar with a wide neck, hand drill, potting soil, pebbles, moss, ferns, lichens, tree seedlings (gathered from the nearest woodland), violet, or African violet, plant

1. Remove the lid of the jar and put it to one side.

2. Lay the jar on its side and cover the bottom with a layer of pebbles. Place a layer of potting soil on top of the pebbles.

3. Starting from the far end of the jar and working toward the neck, plant the various seedlings and plants. The violet will add color to the bottle garden but it does not matter if you do not have one.

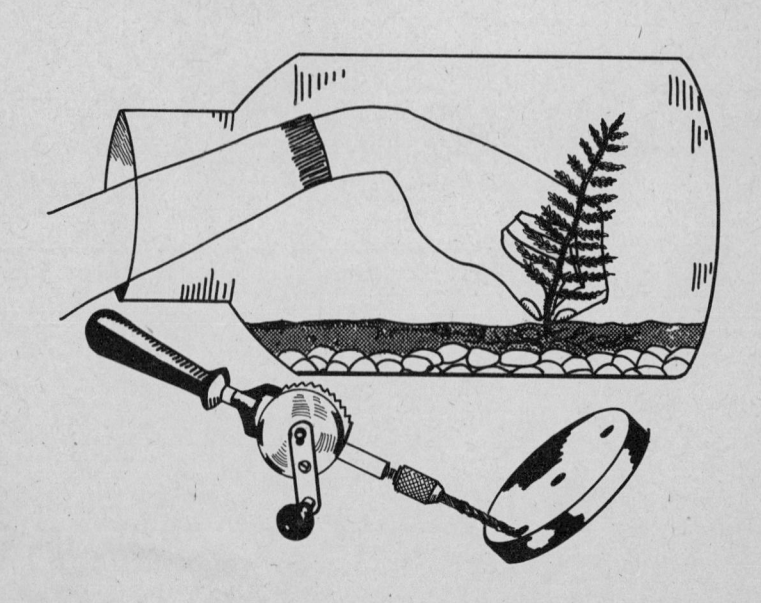

4. Press the soil down firmly around the plants and cover the spaces in between with a layer of moss. If you are unable to find moss, use grass seed instead.

5. Drill a few air holes in the lid of the jar. Moisten the soil by pouring a little water into the jar — this will spread through the pebbles to the far end — and replace the lid.

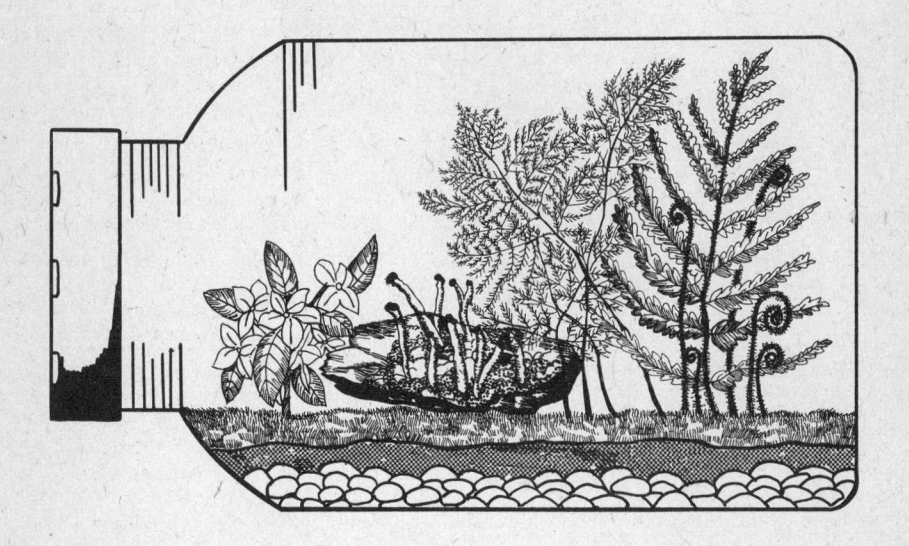

Put the jar in a light place but not in direct sunlight. Keep the soil moist. Water will collect on the glass inside the jar and run back down into the soil again so you will not have to water the bottle garden very often.

# Making things grow out of doors

## Window boxes

You need:
softwood 6 x ¾ inches wide and three times the length of your windowsill, oval wire nails 1½ inches long, hammer, saw, ruler, pencil, oil-based paint, hand drill

1. Measure the length of your windowsill and check that it is at least 6 inches wide.

2. Saw off three equal lengths of wood, each one 5 inches shorter than the length of the windowsill. Then saw off two pieces 7½ inches long for the ends of the box.

3. Drill several large drainage holes in one of the long pieces of wood, forming the bottom of the box.

4. Nail the other two long pieces of wood along the sides of the bottom piece so that they form a 'U' shape. Nail the two smaller pieces across the ends to form a trough.

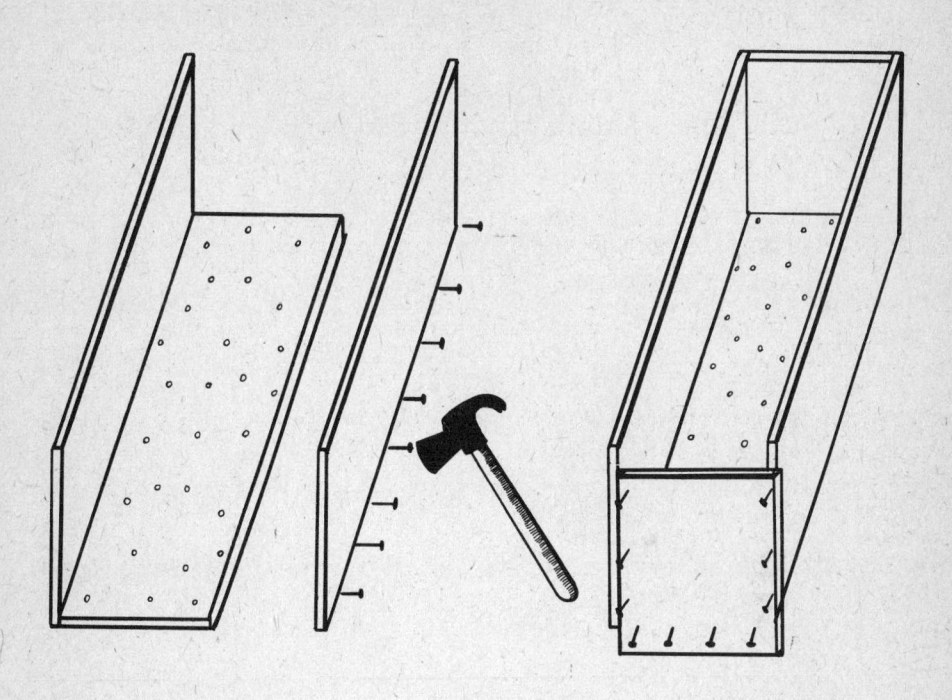

5. Paint the box all over, inside and out, with two coats of a dull-colored paint.

When the paint has dried, put a layer of broken clay pot or pebbles in the bottom of the box, and place the box on the windowsill, supported on two small blocks of wood. Fill the box with potting soil. You can plant bulbs or seedlings in the box just as you can in a garden.

**Preparing the ground**

If you live in a house with a garden, ask your parents to let you have a small area in which to grow your own plants.

Unless the ground has already been prepared for planting, you must first remove all the weeds which would otherwise prevent the plants from growing. Many weeds have underground stems called "rhizomes," and you should try to pull out as many as possible by hand.

The best time to dig the garden is when the soil is fairly moist and crumbly. Make sure that you dig to the full depth of the spade or fork. Turn the soil over, break up the large lumps with the spade, and remove the rest of the weeds as you come across them.

When you have finished digging, rake the surface of the soil to make it fine and level. If you rake from one side of the patch to the other, you will find that all the large stones will collect along one edge and these can be used to make an attractive border.

Gardens are best dug twice a year; once in the autumn, to remove dead plants and loosen the soil before winter frosts, and again in the spring to prepare the ground for planting.

Now you are ready to plant seedlings and young plants in your garden. All the tools you will need for your own patch of garden — forks, watering can, rake, spade, and hoe — are shown on the opposite page.

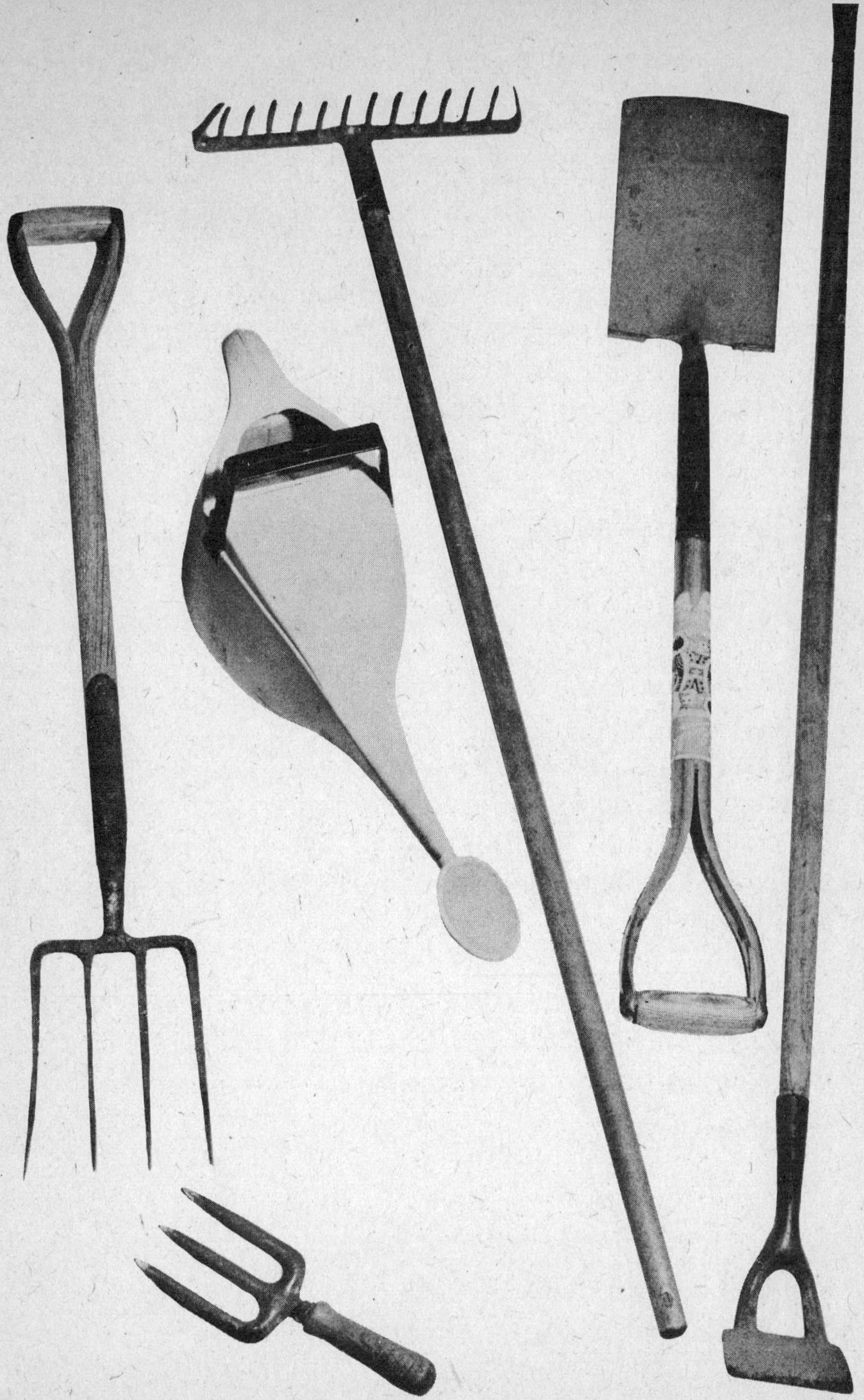

**Weed garden**

The easiest plants to grow are weeds which flourish without any human help. Mark off an area of your garden with a border of stones and leave it undisturbed. You will be amazed at the number and variety of weeds that will soon appear. See how many you can identify.

**Flower garden**

The most popular type of garden is one that contains a variety of colorful flowers. It is important, if you want your display to be impressive, to plan the position of all the different plants in advance.

First draw a plan of your garden on a sheet of graph paper. Shade areas with colored pencils to help you decide where to put the different types of plants. Use the squares to help you plan designs. Arrange the plants according to size, with the larger varieties at the back (possibly against a wall) and the small border plants along the front edge. You can even arrange the seeds of the border plants so that they will spell out your name when they grow.

Most garden flowers can be raised from seeds. They can be grown first indoors in seed trays and then transplanted to the garden in the early summer as described on page 28. If you plant the seeds directly in the garden you must wait until the weather is warm, when all chance of frost is past, otherwise the seedlings may die.

On pages 60-61 is a list of plants that are suitable for your garden. Choose varieties that bloom at different times of the year so that your garden is always in flower. The seed packet will give you this information.

If you want your plants to grow in neat rows, especially where they form a border display, push two sticks into the ground at each end of the row and tie a piece of string tightly between them (see below). Next make a shallow groove along this line with a pencil and sprinkle the seeds evenly along its length. Cover the seeds with a thin layer of soil. Remove the string, but leave the sticks where they are. Push the empty seed packet onto one of the sticks to help you identify the seedlings when they grow.

Seedlings should be replanted fairly close together in the garden, not only because the display will look more beautiful, but also because the weeds will have greater difficulty in finding somewhere to grow. Any weeds that do grow can easily be removed by carefully hoeing between the plants. Use a short, slicing movement with the blade of the hoe just below the surface of the ground. You should keep the soil moist by watering it thoroughly.

Your plants may be one of three kinds:

Annuals: These plants flower for one year only, then die, unless they reseed themselves.

Biennials: These last for two years. They produce only leaves and roots in the first year and flowers the next year.

Perennials: These plants last for three or more years, flowering every year.

Each autumn you should remove the dead annuals. Leave the others undisturbed. When the perennials begin to take up a lot of room you can dig them up in the spring, split them into smaller clumps, and replant them.

Opposite is a plan of a small garden patch and a drawing of the well-balanced garden it grew into, with a climbing rose and taller plants against the wall at the back.

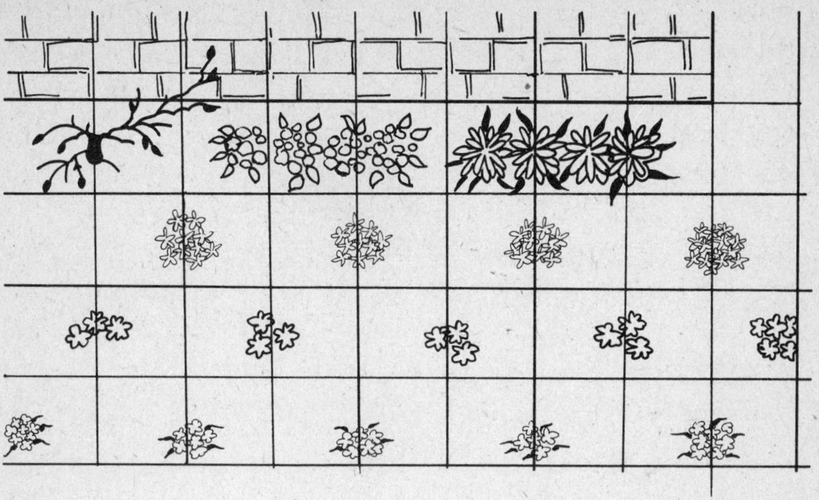

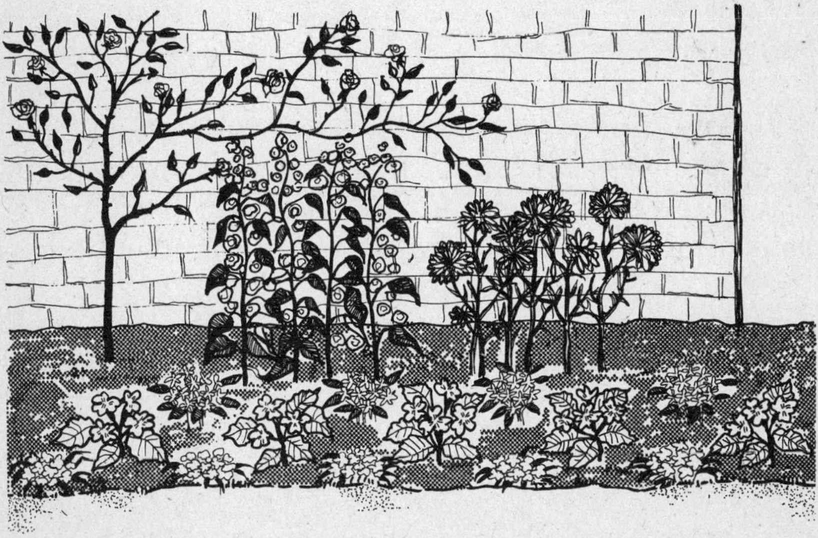

## Vegetable garden

Many of the vegetables and herbs that you see in supermarkets can easily be grown from seed in your patch of garden. Follow the instructions on pages 24-25.

Here are some ideas for making vegetable growing more fun:

Squashes: If your friends can be persuaded to grow them too, you could hold a "biggest squash" contest. Start the seeds off in pots and transplant them. Feed the soil well by digging in plenty of compost before you plant the seeds or seedlings. Allow space for the vines to trail. (Pages 56-57 tell you how to make a compost heap.)

Beans: Climbing varieties need long poles or sticks around which they can wind as they grow. If you plant a row of them you can hold a "bean Olympics" to see which one wins the race to the top.

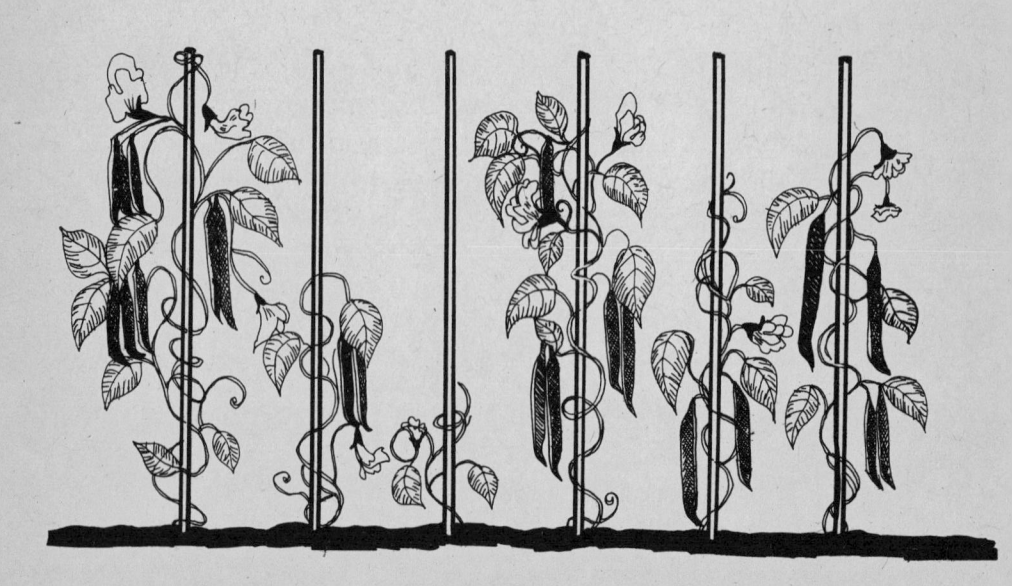

Potatoes: How many potatoes can you get from one plant? For the best results, use seed potatoes planted in holes about 1 foot apart. When shoots appear above the surface, use a trowel to build up the earth in ridges around the stems so that more potatoes have room to form. When the stalks of the plants go yellow, the new potatoes will have formed underground. Lift each plant with a fork and see how many potatoes have grown around the roots.

Other vegetables that are easy to grow are: broccoli, onions, cabbage, brussels sprouts, carrots, lettuce, peas, tomatoes, and cucumbers. In each case follow the instructions on the seed packets.

Keep one section of your garden for herbs such as parsley, thyme, chives, sage, basil, rosemary, tarragon, marjoram, and fennel. Grow them in clumps so that they are easily picked and make sure you label them clearly. If you want to grow mint, plant it in an old bucket with holes in the bottom. This will stop the roots from spreading too far.

## Hanging garden

You need:
old lampshade frame, wire netting, potting soil, large screw hook, strong string, sphagnum moss (from a garden shop), pliers

1. Cut the wire netting with the pliers so that it fits inside the lampshade frame, covering the narrow end. You need not cut an exact shape because the wire can easily be bent, and it does not matter if it overlaps in places.

2. Place a layer of sphagnum moss around the inside of the wire netting to form a dish-shaped lining in the frame. Fill the frame with potting soil.

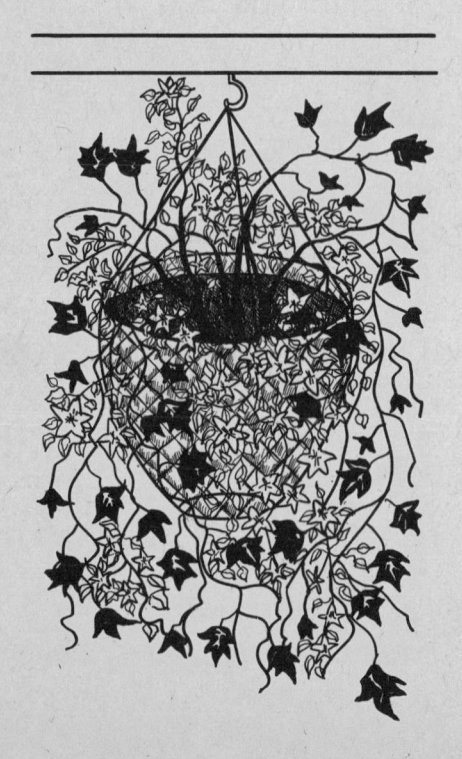

3. Put the seedlings of trailing plants into the potting soil and water them in well. You could use variegated ivy, trailing lobelia, wandering Jew, petunias, star-of-Bethlehem, and others.

4. Tie three equal lengths of strong string together at one end and tie the other ends to the top of the basket so that it will hang level. (See illustration opposite page.)

5. Screw the hook into a wooden arch or porch so that the basket will hang freely.

As the plants grow, they will trail over the sides of the basket, producing a colorful cascade. You could hang the wire frame inside an old sunhat or basket to make it even more colorful.

# Hints for outdoor gardens

**Improving the soil**

To get the best from your garden, you must take as much care of your soil as you do of your plants.

Not all soils are alike in quality. Loam is the ideal, containing a perfect mixture of sand, clay, chalk, and humus. You may, however, find that your garden has too much of one of these and not enough of the others. Chalky and sandy soils dry out very quickly, losing their minerals at the same time. To enable this type of soil to hold water better, and to replace the minerals that have been washed away, you should dig in plenty of compost. Soils with too much clay become water-logged in wet weather and crack open when it is very dry. Drainage can be improved by digging in lime and sieved ashes from a fire.

All types of soil can be improved by adding humus (which consists of dead and decayed animal and plant matter) to lighten the soil and provide more food for growing plants. You can collect humus in the woods or buy it from garden shops.

**Making a compost heap**

Pile all the dead plants, weeds, and grass cuttings from your garden, together with vegetable waste from the kitchen, neatly in one corner of the garden. Bacteria will slowly turn this waste material into valuable compost.

Build up the compost heap in layers, and always take compost from the bottom of the pile for digging into the soil. Composting can be speeded up by adding a thin sprinkling of lime between the layers or by using an "activator" which can be bought at a florist's or nursery.

## Using fertilizers

As plants grow, they use up the mineral salts of the soil. If you grew the same plants year after year without replacing these salts, the soil would slowly become barren. Nitrogen, phosphates, and potash are the most important of these minerals, and they can be added to the soil by using a compound fertilizer bought from a florist's or nursery.

### Getting rid of pests and diseases

Many small creatures, such as aphids and red spider mite, live by feeding on both indoor and outdoor plants.

It is important to give your plants a careful inspection every so often, especially the undersides of the leaves, to make sure these pests have not gathered there. If they do appear in large numbers, spray or powder the leaves with insecticides from a garden supplier. Follow the instructions very carefully because some of the insecticides can be harmful to human beings and pets.

Many pests that live in the soil, such as slugs and snails, may also harm your plants. They may either eat the roots or crawl up the stems and eat the leaves. Again, garden suppliers will advise you as to which insecticide will be most suitable, but you can help by killing any of these pests that you come across while digging and weeding.

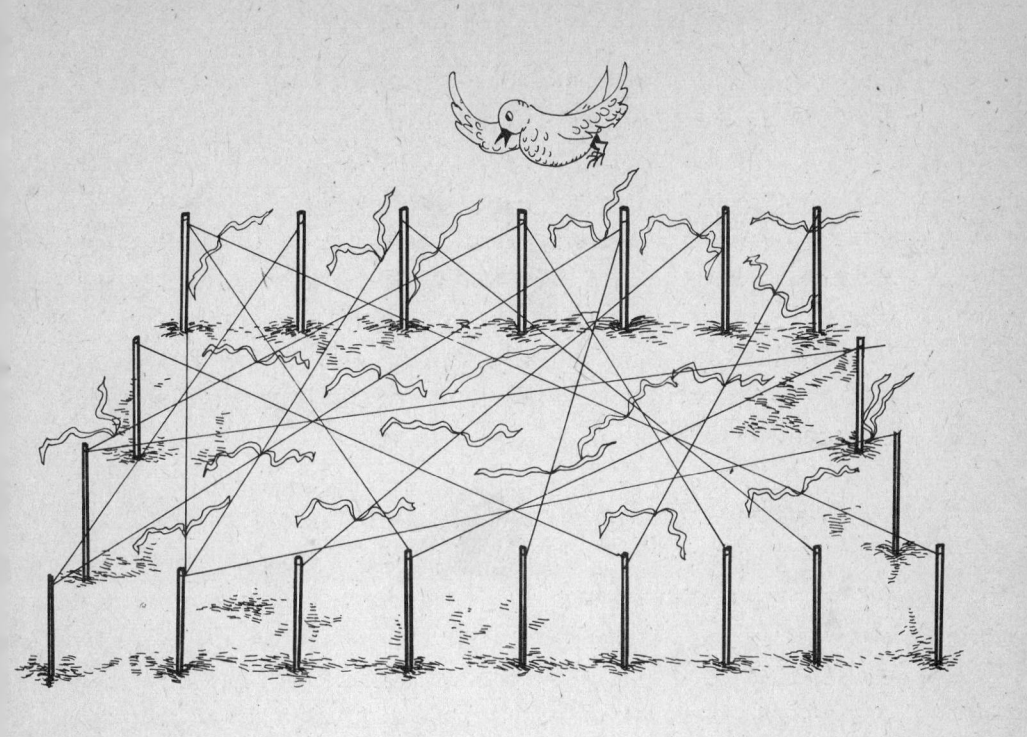

Birds may be just as destructive in your garden as insects, especially at seed-planting time. They will scratch below the thin covering of soil and eat the seeds before they have a chance to grow. You can prevent this from happening by placing short sticks all around the seed patch and then string black thread between the sticks and over the seed bed, rather like a spider's web. If birds are still attracted to the seed bed, hang strips of aluminum foil from the thread. The wind will blow the strips about, and the movement and noise will frighten birds away.

## Flowers to grow from seeds

| Flower | Color(s) | Type |
| --- | --- | --- |
| Ageratum | blue | annual |
| Alyssum | white | annual |
| Aster | various | annual |
| Aubrieta | pink/mauve | perennial |
| Canterbury Bell | blue | biennial |
| *Carnation | various | perennial |
| *Chrysanthemum | various | perennial |
| Clarkia | various | annual |
| Cornflower (Batchelor's Buttons) | blue | annual |
| Cosmos | various | annual |
| Dahlia | various | perennial |
| Daisy | various | perennial |
| Delphinium | blue/white | perennial |
| Foxglove | various | biennial |
| Geum | orange/red | ann./peren. |
| Godetia | reds | annual |
| Gypsophila | white | ann./peren. |
| Hollyhock | various | perennial |
| Larkspur | various | annual |
| Lobelia | blue/white | annual |
| Lupin | various | perennial |
| Marigold | orange/yellow | annual |
| Nasturtium | orange/yellow | annual |

| Flower | Color(s) | Type |
| --- | --- | --- |
| *Nemesia | various | annual |
| Nigella (Love-in-a-mist) | various | annual |
| Pansy | various | ann./bien. |
| Petunia | various | annual |
| *Phlox | various | annual |
| *Pinks | various | perennial |
| *Primroses | various | perennial |
| Poppy | various | annual |
| *Salvia | red | annual |
| Scabiosa | mauve | annual |
| Snapdragons | various | annual |
| Stock | various | annual |
| Sunflower | various | annual |
| Sweet pea | various | annual |
| Sweet William | various | ann./bien. |
| Wallflower | orange/yellow | biennial |
| Zinnia | various | annual |

* these flowers are best grown as indoor seedlings and then transplanted to the garden

# Index

annuals, 50

beans, 12, 13, 15, 17, 52
biennials, 50
birds, 59
bottle garden, 42-43
bulbs, 20-23

carnation, 6
compost heap, 56-57
corms, 22, 23
crocus, 23
cuttings, 28

desert, 38-39
diseases, 58

experiments, 5-19

fertilizers, 57
flower garden, 48-49
flowers from seeds, 60-61
freesias, 22
fruit pits, 27

gardening tools, 47
geotropism, 13
geranium, 8-9, 14, 28
gladioli, 22
grass seed, 30
"green hair," 30

hanging garden, 54-55
house plants, 32-33
hyacinths, 20, 22
hydrotropism, 13

improving soil, 56

miniature desert, 38-39
miniature garden, 34-37
mustard farm, 26

narcissus, 22

osmosis, 5

perennials, 50
pests, 58
photosynthesis, 9
phototropism, 14
planting and sowing, 20-29
potatoes, 5, 9, 31, 53
preparing the ground, 46

repotting, 28

seeds, easy to grow, 26, 30
 60-61
snowdrops, 22
soil, 16
soil, improving, 56
soil, types, 56
sowing seeds, 24-25
squashes, 52

tools, 47
transpiration, 7
transplanting, 28
tulips, 23

underwater garden, 40-41

vegetable garden, 52-53

water weed, 10, 40-41
weed garden, 48
window boxes, 44-45

# Notes about my garden

# Notes about my garden